GHETTO
For Sale

A Tourist Story

Through the eyes of the tourist, GHETTO documents the journey of an American family's convergence with an Iranian refugee family fleeing persecution and resettling in Venice, Italy. As the narrative progresses toward its sister refugee narrative (begin at reverse cover), it depicts the American family's enriched understanding of what it means to engage with diverse cultures in an effort to create a community where global citizenship is embraced.

Refugee Narrative

Read Right to Left
Begin at Black Cover

Manifesto

Tourist Narrative

Read Left to Right
Begin at White Cover

We're finally on vacation, my love.

Cheers!

My favorite art installation!

At last, we meet in-person.

Honey, where's your bracelet?

It must have fallen into the water...

Maybe we should find another hotel.

Wait, why?

Well, we didn't come here to visit the Middle East, and I just don't think it's a good influence on you kids.

Oh, come on, Dad. You always complain about spending money.

Now you want to turn down free accommodation and go to an expensive hotel without a reservation all because of some refugees?

Honey, your father has a point. I don't know if our values are the same as theirs.

They are HUMAN, just like us.

Your dad and I just want to be careful.

We don't know anything about these people.

Maybe we should at least stay a few nights to see how we feel.

We owe it to the Powells.

Maybe we should come back later...

Wait, why?

Wait, we are leaving. Please use the pool as you like!

Oh...

Okay, thank you.

I can't believe I lost my favorite bracelet. It was quite valuable.

It's just a bracelet, Mom.

What's wrong, honey?

Look around us.

We're surrounded by people who left everything they had to be here. What right do we have to complain?

I'm sorry, it's just that hearing the stories of the refugees here makes me grateful for what we have.

I see...

...Honey, the world can be an awful place, but don't let it get you down.

I won't.

There must be something I can do to help.

I want to be part of the solution.

When I heard about Laleh's journey to Venice...

... she inspired me. I want to be as strong as she is.

GHETTO NUOVO

...A sudden influx of Jewish refugees prompted the Venetian government to implement segregation policies in 1516.

Thus, the Ghetto Nuovo, the original Jewish ghetto, was created. Here's one of the original synagogues.

The Republic forced the Jewish people to live in an area where the foundries were once located. In Venetian, foundries were known as geti.

Perhaps this is where the word "ghetto" comes from.

THE GHETTO NUOVO, ON THE ONE HAND, PROVIDED THE JEWISH PEOPLE A PLACE OF THEIR OWN.

IT WAS A PLACE WHERE THEY COULD PRACTICE THEIR FAITH FREE FROM PHYSICAL PERSECUTION.

ON THE OTHER HAND, THEY WERE OBLIGATED TO WEAR A VISIBLE SYMBOL OF THEIR ETHNIC IDENTIFICATION.

THIS PERPETUATED THEIR SEGREGATION, FURTHERING PREJUDICES AND STIGMAS.

JEWISH RESIDENTS OF THE VENETIAN GHETTO WERE CONFINED TO SPECIFIC TRADES--THE CITY IMPOSED UPON THEM A STRICT CURFEW.

WITHIN VENICE, THEY WERE SECOND-CLASS CITIZENS.

After centuries of push-and-pull between acceptance and expulsion, the Jewish ghetto's residents were eventually accepted into Venetian society-- the prejudices and stigmas have dissolved.

Yeah, but this kind of stuff is still happening all over the world...

GHETTO

"How will we live together?"

The theme of the 2021 Venice Architecture Biennale, "How will we live together?" encourages individuals to consider the role of the architect in creating spaces for inclusion, questioning the architect's role as a "cordial convener and a custodian of the spatial contract". GHETTO, our theoretical project, imagines a physical conduit for the redistribution of wealth from tourists to refugees by transferring the equity garnered in the development process in a mutually beneficial manner. While this project explores one iteration of this redistribution model, it can be applied across a variety of geographies, scales and contexts to provide a myriad of social benefits.

In the effort to explore the responsibility as global citizens, to care for one another, and to find mutually beneficial financial mechanisms that redistribute equity to provide social benefits, GHETTO is a theoretical series of four architectural islands that demonstrate these intentions through their economic model. Each of the islands are positioned near one of four compelling sites: the Venetian ghetto, Stazione di Santa Lucia, Piazza San Marco, and the Arsenale. These sites were carefully selected to parallel four key-influencing factors in Venice: the Jewish ghetto as project inspiration, the refugee crisis, Venetian over-tourism, and challenging the traditional role of the architect.

Through the project, Henriquez Partners, in collaboration with the UNHCR, aspires to spark meaningful dialogue about the issues affecting all cities and our collective obligation to create inclusive and engaged communities where all are welcome and belong.

GHETTO is Henriquez Partners Architects' project for the European Cultural Center's invitational exhibition in Venice, TIME SPACE EXISTENCE, during the 2021 Architecture Biennale.

Manifesto

This theoretical architectural project proposes the provision of housing for refugees funded through a condominium timeshare model. The intention is to illustrate the power of the role of the architect in the creation of inclusive cities. The specific goal is to share a framework which leverages the power of the development community to provide social benefit to others who have less.

The Jewish ghetto in Cannaregio embodies a latent history which challenges Venice's tradition as an inclusive city. Approaches to the contemporary refugee crisis must encourage inclusivity, cultural resiliency, identity, and dignity without ghettoization.

Image: Andrea Wyner

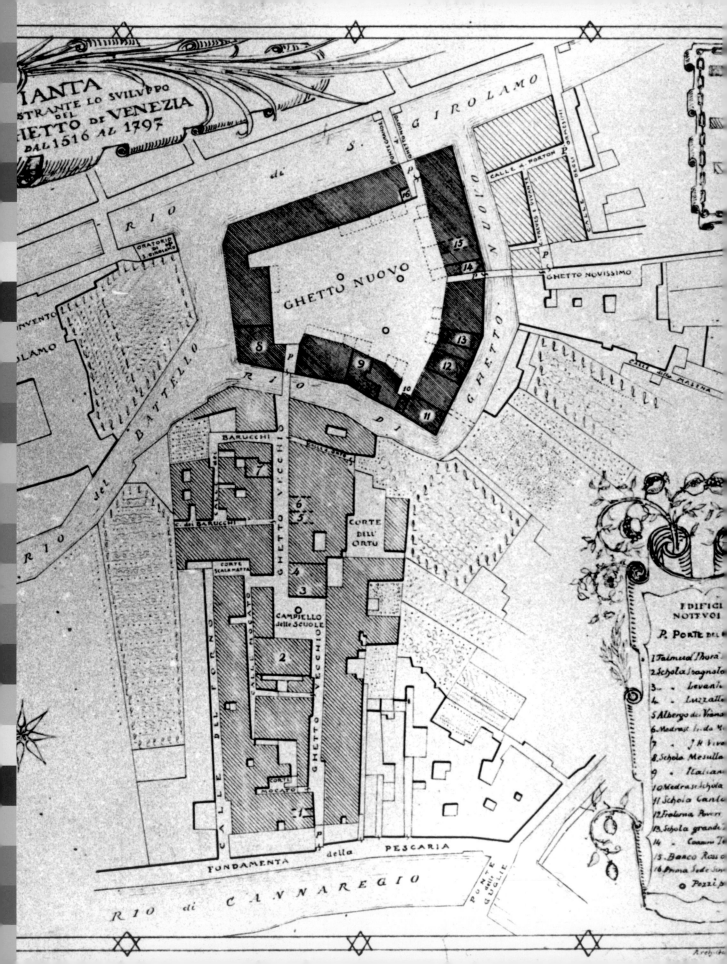

PIANTA
MOSTRANTE LO SVILUPPO
DEL
GHETTO DI VENEZIA
DAL 1516 AL 1797

RIO di S. GIROLAMO

ORATORIO DI S. GIROLAMO

RIO del BATTELLO

CONVENTO

GIROLAMO

RIO

CALLE 4. PORTON

GHETTO NUOVO

GHETTO NOVISSIMO

GHETTO NOVISSIMO

8

P

9

10

11

12

13

14

15

16

GHETTO DI GHETTO

CALLE della MALENA

BARUCCHI

C. dei BARUCCHI

CORTE SCALA MATTA

GHETTO VECCHIO

CALLE del FORNO

CALLE DEL FORNO

CAMPIELLO delle SCUOLE

CORTE DELL' ORTO

CORTE MOCATO

7

6

5

4

3

2

1

CALLE DEL FORNO

GHETTO VECCHIO

FONDAMENTA della PESCARIA

PONTE GUGLIE

RIO di CANNAREGIO

EDIFICI NOTEVOLI

P. PORTE DEL

1 Talmud Thora
2 Schola Spagnola
3   " Levant
4   " Luzzatto
5 Albergo di Viani
6 Medrasi fondo
7   " J H Viv
8 Schola Mesulla
9   " Italian
10 Medrase Schola
11 Schola Canto
12 Fraterna Povei
13 Schola grande
14   " Coanim
15 Banco Rosso
16 Prima Sede
o Pozzi

Preface

Gregory Henriquez

In collaboration with UNHCR and the ECC, Henriquez Partners Architects imagines GHETTO, an architectural project which proposes the resettlement of 1,000 refugees into Venice financed by the sale of time-share condominiums for tourists from America.

The inspiration for the project came from the site of the ECC exhibition in Palazzo Mora located in Cannaregio, home of the Jewish ghetto, and our desire to illustrate our studio's credo that architecture has the potential to be a poetic expression of social justice.

In the 16th century, an influx of Jewish arrivals into Venice led to a civic response that forced the Jews into mandatory, segregated living quarters, which became the first ghetto in history. Our project considers a related, contemporary situation within the global refugee crisis but searches for an inclusive model of development.

If the role of the architect is to transcend that of a mere consultant for hire, then as true professionals, we share together a duty to identify and facilitate opportunities for achieving social good.

Our Vancouver studio designs complex mixed-use projects that aspire to integrate ethics and poetics to create inclusive and engaged communities. Our role as a metaphorical and architectural "Robin Hood" relies on complex rezoning with economies of scale that enable the development community to meet their financial objectives in tandem with a necessary transfer of equity towards socially valuable objectives.

Our project's intention is to encourage a meaningful dialogue about the relationship between citizens and cities in a global context. What does it mean to be a "citizen"? What is a city's inherent accountability to an individual's humanity? What is the role of the architect in building an inclusive city?

In this theoretical development model for Venice, the city's historical saturation of tourists is leveraged as an economic opportunity to house refugees in need. The GHETTO development proposes a timeshare model funded by tourists that provides a housing mix of temporary and permanent settlement, with approximately 2,000 housing units being allotted to both tourists and refugees.

Considering our current global refugee crisis and the serious urban issues that all major cities are and will be confronting after COVID-19, our exhibit explores the leadership role of the architect in inclusive city building that is financially viable and encourages the values of inclusivity, diversity, and social justice in the creation of places where we all belong.

Image: © The Oster Visual Documentation Center,
ANU – Museum of the Jewish People

Intentions

GHETTO is a theoretical project that explores the role of the architect in the creation of inclusive citizen cities by providing housing for Iranian refugees funded through an innovative timeshare model, leveraging American tourist dollars to provide social benefit in the form of refugee housing in Venice. The project explores the role of the architect and that of all citizens collectively establishing a model of architecture which transfers wealth to those in need while creating a beneficial outcome for every individual involved.

Inclusivity

To acknowledge the issue of segregation in city-planning and to propose inclusive alternatives

Advocacy

To demonstrate the architect's role in advocating for inclusive city building; to draw attention to the UNHCR and the work they do globally regarding the resettlement of refugees

Belonging

To welcome the refugee as a citizen of the world and provide resources for re-establishing a new form of inclusive community. Nation-states must dissolve in order to face humanitarian crises.

Facilitation

To facilitate a discussion about ability versus obligation in a world where a privileged few hold a majority of the wealth and how the model of transferring equity from profitable sectors towards socially valuable objectives can be leveraged

Characters

Within the theoretical architectural project in Venice, each intention is explored in narratives through the lenses of four main "citizens" of the GHETTO:

GHETTO Resident

ghet· to | res· i· dent | noun

A resident of a quarter of the city of Venice in which Jews were formerly required to live segregated from society; a member of a minority group living in a designated area primarily because of social, legal, or economic pressure

Refugee

ref· u· gee | noun

A person who is forced to flee their country to escape danger or persecution; a person who seeks refuge

Tourist

tour· ist | noun

A person who travels or visits a place for pleasure

Architect

ar· chi· tect | noun

A person who navigates the intersection of justice and beauty and of ethics and aesthetics, creating communities that encourage inclusivity

"Contemporary architecture is often revered purely as an aesthetic rather than as a social force. The architect, as a navigator, has a leadership role in pursuing the meaningful intersection of justice and beauty, of ethics and aesthetics. In the creation of communities that encourage values of inclusivity, diversity and social benefit, the architect's role has the potential to facilitate a transfer of equity to those most in need."

— Gregory Henriquez

GHETTO Resident

"What is a city's inherent accountability to an individual's humanity?"

Story of Exodus

Exodus is the story of Israelites enslaved in Egypt, their liberation through their God, Yahweh, revelations that they received near Mount Sinai, and their passage through the wilderness to the borders of Canaan. The story of Exodus is central to Judaism and is recounted frequently in Jewish prayers and commemorated in festivals such as Passover. The narrative also resonates with non-Jewish groups, from African Americans striving for freedom and civil rights to contemporary refugees enduring great hardship to find a welcoming place to call home. It is one of the most influential stories in the history of humanity.

Image: Harvard Map Collection, Harvard Library

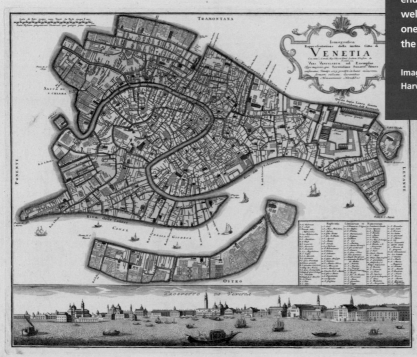

The Jewish ghetto in Cannaregio embodies a latent history which challenges Venice's tradition as an inclusive city. The ghetto offers a duality; born from segregation and prejudice, it inadvertently preserved Jewish culture and offered protection from physical persecution. Today, while Jewish residents live throughout the city, the ghetto remains the heart of Jewish culture in Venice. Approaches to the contemporary refugee crisis must encourage inclusivity, cultural resiliency, identity, and dignity without ghettoization.

GHETTO intends to promote Citizen Cities. The vision of a Citizen City is one that transcends the traditional urban goals of economic stability and working infra-structure, and allows for inclusivity of its people with a variety of economic levels, different cultures, and diverse identities. A Citizen City also provides and encourages open access to democratic and civic engagement, and develops cultural facilities and promotes cultural identity, thus enhancing a sense of community. Diversity, inclusivity, and civic engage-ment represent the true "richness" of an urban center and can provide the basis for cultural sustainability: this is a Citizen City.

The Refugee

"What does it mean to be a citizen?"

Unlike immigrants, refugees do not leave their country of origin by choice, nor is there an option to return. It is critical that when refugees arrive in a new country they have support and a sense of safety.

In 2020, over 1.4 million refugees needed resettlement globally. Over 70.8 million people have been forcibly displaced worldwide. Over the last five years, the number of refugees requiring global resettlement has doubled while resettlement opportunities have decreased by 50% leaving only 1% of refugees with legal access to resettlement. No single solution will resolve this immense challenge; it is our collective responsibility.

65.6 M
Forcibly displaced people worldwide in 2017

1%
Percentage of refugees having access to settlement services

1M+
Number of refugees have been resettled in the last 25 years

Image: UNHCR Media Library

"Multiculturalism strengthens the Canadian political, economic, and social system. Multiculturalism has given Canada a reputation and an international image that we are in the vanguard of acknowledging and managing a national and global reality where cultural diversity is flourishing." — Ho Hon Leung

"Everyone has the right to seek and to enjoy in other countries asylum from persecution."

— Article 14 – UN Declaration of Human Rights – Fundamental Human Rights

Image: UNHCR Media Library

The Tourist

"How can tourism be more sustainable?"

Venice receives approximately €2 billion in revenue from 20 million tourists per year. 76% of tourists are "day trippers" who make very small contributions to the local economy. Although often depicted as villains, global tourists are major economic contributors to a Venetian population that now depends upon tourism for its livelihood.

Tourism has the potential to be a major economic stimulator to a population that depends on it, but only if tourists are encouraged to vacation via more sustainable means. Organizations such as Venezia Autentica offer experiences that guide tourist expenditures toward activities ranging from supporting artists of dying Venetian crafts to booking private tours with a local. Shifting tourist habits toward sustainable tourism benefits both vacationers and the local community.

A timeshare in GHETTO is a capital investment, which encourages long stays and repeating visitors who develop a relationship with the city of Venice and its community. The model provides annual recurring sustainable revenue and more meaningful contributions to the local economy.

19€

Average expenditure of a day-tripper in Venice

23€

Average expenditure of a tourist staying more than 2 nights in Venice

22 hrs

Current average stay in Venice

Approximately 76% of the 20 million tourists come just for the day, straining rather than strengthening the Venetian economy and infrastructure.

"The vision of a Citizen City is one that transcends the traditional urban goals of economic stability and working infrastructure, and allows for inclusivity of its people, with a variety of economic levels, different cultures, and diverse identities. A Citizen City also provides and encourages open access to democratic and civic engagement, and develops cultural facilities and promotes cultural identity, thus enhancing a sense of community." — Marya Cotten Gould

"Venezia Autentica is a social enterprise founded in Venice in 2017. Our goal is to transform the way tourism impacts the city. We want to move from an unsustainable mass tourism, that benefits neither the visitors nor the residents, to a more sustainable, more responsible tourism which is a true win-win.

To do so, we are using social innovation and digital technologies to make it easy and fun for visitors to have a quality experience in Venice while making a positive impact locally. With our campaigns, platforms and programs, we empower both local businesses and travelers by creating a system that bridges the gap between them. Visitors can therefore have a more authentic and more meaningful experience that directly supports local businesses. This is important as it benefits the quality of tourism and the local economy and helps to preserve the local community, culture, identity and environment."

veneziaautentica.com
Photo property of Venezia Autentica

"Architects can serve as facilitators of relationships. The development of relationships among all sectors, such as private developers, government agencies, and community organizations, allows the architect to build a credible reputation that can be employed to encourage the consideration of a broader spectrum of social interests in his or her projects. While not every goal can be achieved in every project, most projects have elements that allow for the encouragement of strategies to achieve greater urban inclusivity."

— Marya Cotten Gould

The Architect / A Transfer of Equity

"Does obligation come with ability?"

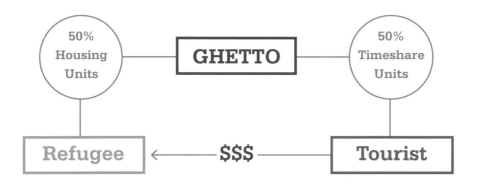

GHETTO challenges the traditional role of the architect, promoting all architects and citizens to collectively establish a model of architecture that transfers wealth to those in need while creating a beneficial outcome for each individual.

The mechanism for the redistribution of capital is a timeshare model that provides accommodation for both refugees and tourists. This process is inspired by the inclusive development process which leverages contributions (CAC's) in the City of Vancouver, British Columbia.

Within GHETTO, timeshare units are to be sold to tourists in one-week increments, raising capital that funds the provision of units for refugees who are seeking asylum or resettlement. Within this intervention, half of the units are provided for refugees, and the other half for tourists. Understanding that typical timeshares have an 80% occupancy, we also imagine that the 20% of the timeshare stock that is unused could be made available for refugees who have a shorter term and immediate need for housing upon arrival.

Community Amenity Contributions (CAC's) are significant cash contributions provided by property developers when the City of Vancouver grants development rights through a rezoning process which increases density, thereby placing increased demand on city facilities and public amenities.

Development Model

"Indeed the distribution of wealth is too important an issue to be left to the economists, sociologists, historians, and philosophers." — Thomas Piketty

The proforma illustrates in detail how the development model is able to fund refugee units through timeshare sales. The sales of GHETTO's 1,000 timeshare condominiums funds 100% of the 1,000 refugee units, fulfilling our break-even/non-profit mandate. The cost of each living unit provides equal access to shared amenities between tourists and refugees as well as amenities purposed specifically for either the tourist or the refugee.

The development model explores how the role of the architect can assist in bringing awareness to global citizens to feel responsible for caring for one another. It is also a tool to inspire the creation of other mutually beneficial financial mechanisms that redistribute equity to provide social benefit and to shape how we will live together.

Venice Break Even Pro-Forma

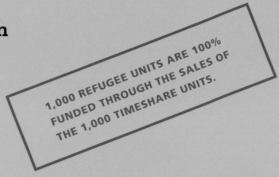

1,000 REFUGEE UNITS ARE 100% FUNDED THROUGH THE SALES OF THE 1,000 TIMESHARE UNITS.

Inputs

Number of Units	2,000
Existing Land Value	Priceless
% of Gross Area for Refugee Housing	50%
% of Gross Area for Timeshare	50%
Gross Area for Refugee Housing (sqm)	71,000
Net Saleable Timeshare (sqm)	71,000
Amenity Space (sqm)	5,000

Assumptions

Hard Costs (Construction)/sqm Refugee Housing	€ 5,000
Hard Costs (Construction)/sqm Timeshare Housing	€ 5,000
Infrastructure Upgrade and Site Servicing	€ 30 Million
Hard Cost (Construction) Contingency	15%
Permitting	€ 1 Million
Management Fee % of Hard Costs	5%
Construction Soft Costs	18%
Timeshare Weeks	52
Timeshare Units	1,000
Time Share Studio Average Price/per Unit	€ 22,000
Marketing Costs	2.5%
Real Estate Commissions	3%

Break-even Summary – Revenue

Timeshare Revenue	€ 1,144,000,000
Less: Total Commissions (3%)	€ 34,320,000
Less: Management Fee (5%)	€ 35,500,000
NET SALES REVENUE	**€ 1,074,180,000**

Break-even Summary – Costs

Hard Costs – Refugee Housing	€ 355,000,000
Hard Costs – Timeshare Housing	€ 355,000,000
Hard Costs – Contingency	€ 106,500,000
Soft Costs	€ 148,290,476
Rezoning and Infrastructure	€ 31,000,000
Total Build Costs	€ 995,790,476
Marketing Costs	€ 28,600,000
Finance Costs (5% estimate)	€ 49,789,524
Total Costs	€ 1,074,180,000
TOTAL COST OF PROJECT	**€ 1,074,180,000**

Sanctuary Welcome

Our refugee sanctuary provides housing, support services, and community that you need to begin a new life. Whether you need a temporary home to gain stability or need longer-term accommodation, you are welcome to establish yourself and build community within GHETTO.

Why a sanctuary?

GHETTO offers a variety of units ranging from one to three bedrooms to suit refugees coming as single individuals or as families. Shared public amenities, such as a communal kitchen where you may break bread together, encourage social interaction and help to build a sense of community with your fellow residents. Within this sanctuary, we offer both in-person and virtual counseling for victims of torture, a work program for survivors of violence and trauma, family resources for orphans, group support for LGBTQ refugees, and a peer support group for men and women. Our supporting amenities focus on assisting in the preservation of all cultures and pieces of your identity, heritage, and sense of self while you go through a significant life-transition. We know

that leaving your homeland has not been an easy journey or one made by choice. With the help of a variety of non-profit organizations, GHETTO provides extensive settlement, language, mental health, and employment services to help you establish your new home in Venice.

A sense of community is one of the most important factors in successful resettlement; GHETTO provides you with the tools, connections, and resources to help you become part of a new diverse community within Italy.

How does it work?

Through both the asylum and refugee application processes, you automatically qualify for housing and services within GHETTO, and the GHETTO Housing Corporation automatically registers you to provide housing to you and your family. Upon entering GHETTO's community, our welcome center will connect you with each of our support services. This will assist you in procedures such as petitioning for your spouse and children to join you, obtaining travel documents, and applying for permanent residence.

REFUGEE SUPPORT – Our 24-7 support team is always available to assist you, providing you support throughout your entire resettlement journey.

Timeshare Opportunity

Venice, home of the gondolier, grand canals, and St. Mark's Basilica, is one of the most visited sites in the world. Experience it like a local by investing in a timeshare.

Why invest in a timeshare?

Timeshare ownership offers every benefit of owning your own vacation home without any of the responsibilities. Unlike typical hotels, GHETTO suites and studios include comforts to make you feel at home, such as fully equipped kitchens and private laundry facilities. You will also have access to a range of amenities designed to help you engage with locals such as cooking classes, Italian language classes, locally tailored excursions and a concierge service. While purchasing a timeshare is not a money-maker, it is a cost-saver. This investment is far less expensive than a hotel, yet it includes access to numerous amenities and an extended family waiting to greet you upon your every return. GHETTO timeshares are a socially responsible travel option that offers you an authentic experience within Venice while helping those most in need. The equity raised through the timeshares is used to support housing for refugees. In taking part of the innovative timeshare model, you may rest assured that your investment has provided meaningful housing and services for those displaced against their will. By encouraging longer stays, your ethical investment also supports local businesses, and the overall livelihood of Venetians.

How does it work?

A one-time capital investment of €12,500 – €25,000 provides you with a deeded luxury vacation accommodation of one week per year for 25 years. You may pick the week that fits your schedule based on availability or elect to have a guaranteed fixed week per year. Should you find yourself unable to use your timeshare week, no problem! You may donate your unused week as short-term shelter for refugees in need. In return you will be provided with an eligible Canadian or US donation tax receipt from the GHETTO Housing Corporation while providing much needed shelter to a refugee.

TOURIST INQUIRY – Our 24-7 support team is always here to assist you.

Visit our website at henriquezpartners.com/venice-2021/

Ghetto Nuovo

250 Timeshare Units
250 Refugee Units

1

3 **Stazione Di Santa Lucia**

250 Timeshare Units
250 Refugee Units

2 **Piazza San Marco**

250 Timeshare Units
250 Refugee Units

GHETTO Project Sites

GHETTO is managed by the Canadian non-profit company, the Ghetto Housing Corporation, whose purpose is to provide housing for Iranian refugees through leveraging tourist capital. To capture the equity potential created through the real estate development process, the 2,000-unit development provides 1,000 total units for refugees and 1,000 total units for American tourists fully funded by the tourist time-share model over four different island sites. These four sites were selected to provide a sufficient number of both timeshare and refugee housing units to create a revenue-neutral financial model. Each of these sites is metaphorically associated with one of the key citizens in the making of the development: the Ghetto Nuovo with the civic official, Piazza San Marco with the tourist, the Stazione with the refugee, and the Arsenale with the architect.

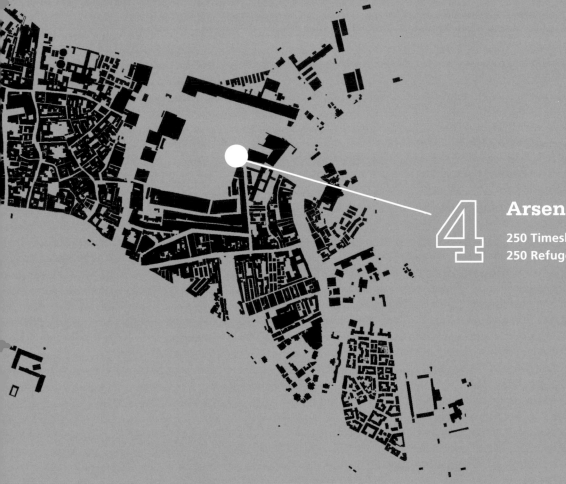

4 Arsenale

250 Timeshare Units
250 Refugee Units

Ghetto Nuovo

One island, comprised of 250 residents, is adjacent to the original Jewish ghetto. This island's location acknowledges the initial inspiration for the entire project.

2 Piazza San Marco

The second island, composed of 250 residents, acknowledges the important role tourism plays in Venice and is adjacent to Piazza San Marco, one of the most popular tourist destinations in the world.

Stazione di Santa Lucia

The third site, comprised of 250 residents, is beside the train station, the main arrival port for refugees coming to Venice.

Arsenale

The fourth site location, composed of 250 residents, is inspired by the role of the architect and is adjacent to the site of the historic Arsenale where the Venice Biennale of Architecture is headquartered.

Rooftop Gardens

Residential Living Units

Public Realm

GHETTO Development Program Elements

Rooftop Gardens

Both refugees and tourists have access to a linear 350-meter elevated outdoor park where they may find solitude within an intimate garden or gather and build community in more expansive areas along the park.

Residential Living Units

The residential units have typical arrangements of 1–4 bedrooms and are occupied interchangeably by refugees and tourists.

Public Realm

The linear public street acts as a horizontal datum and a circulation thoroughfare through the island, GHETTO. The old city of Venice below it accesses the public realm via two points at each end. Each entrance point forms a node: one node for tourists and one node for refugees. At the tourist node, a cluster of tourist-related amenities are located. At the refugee node, a group of refugee-related services are located. Shared amenities for both tourists and refugees are distributed between the two nodes.

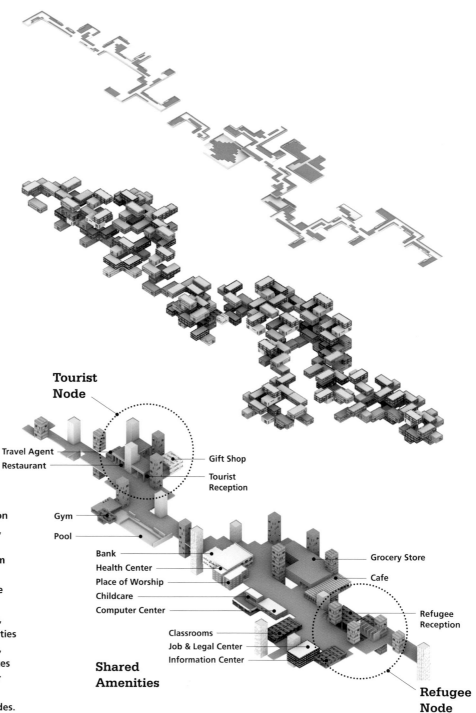

Tourist Node

Travel Agent
Restaurant
Gift Shop
Tourist Reception

Gym
Pool

Bank
Health Center
Place of Worship
Childcare
Computer Center

Grocery Store
Cafe

Refugee Reception

Classrooms
Job & Legal Center
Information Center

Shared Amenities

Refugee Node

GHETTO Floorplans

2 Bedroom Unit

1 bedroom
1 bed + 1 bath unit

€12,500
per week

Upper Level

Lower Level

2 Bedroom
2 Bed + 2.5 Bath

€20,000
per week

Upper Level

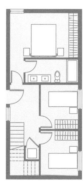

Lower Level

3 Bedroom
3 Bed + 1.5 Bath

€22,500
per week

Upper Level

Lower Level

4 Bedroom
4 Bed + 2 Bath

€25,000
per week

What is a Citizen City?

Marya Cotten Gould, Excerpt from *Citizen City*, 2016

"Good architecture offers societies a place for existential orientation. It allows for participation in meaningful action, conveying to the participant an understanding of his or her place in the world. Successful architecture opens up a clearing for an individual's experience of purpose through participation in cultural institutions." — Alberto Pérez-Gómez

According to the United Nations, more than half of the world's population today, 3.9 billion people, live in urban areas and by 2050, it is estimated that 66 percent of the world's population will be living in cities. Urbanization is a major trend of the 21st century and is a fundamental component in achieving sustainable development as the world's population grows exponentially and the resources of our planet are increasingly constrained. When cities are operating in their ideal sense, they can serve as hubs for commerce, job development, and economic growth as well as centres for innovation, culture, and community.

The vision of a Citizen City is one that transcends the traditional urban goals of economic stability and working infrastructure and allows for inclusivity of its people, with a variety of economic levels, different cultures, and diverse identities. A Citizen City also provides and encourages open access to democratic and civic engagement and develops cultural facilities and promotes cultural identity, thus enhancing a sense of community. Diversity, inclusivity, and civic engagement represent the true "richness" of an urban center and can provide the basis for cultural sustainability: this is a Citizen City.

In *The Just City*, Susan Fainstein champions the concept of a "just city" as an approach to moral urban planning and development that incorporates three central concepts in her conception of justice: equity, democracy, and diversity. She explains why she prefers the term "equity" over "equality":

"The goal of equality is too complex, demanding, and unrealistic to be an objective in the context of capitalist cities. It acts as a magnet for all the objections based on rewards to the most deserving, on questions of the obliteration of incentives, on the trade-off between growth and equality, and on the unfairness of penalizing everyone above the median in the name of the greater good."

Equity, Fainstein argues, is a term that connotes fairness, which is a broader-appealing and less inflammatory term politically than equality. Fairness is more achievable normative value to be striving for in urban planning, particularly in a North American market economy. According to Fainstein, equity "refers to a distribution of both material and non-material benefits derived from public policy that does not favor those already better off at the beginning." This means that the disadvantaged should be taken into account in making urban planning decisions as a form of redistributive justice. Making public policy decisions from a pro-equity standpoint means that outcomes of those decisions should be evaluated in accordance with the distribution of those benefits. A simple example would be allocating funding for the improvement of a community center in a traditionally underserved neighborhood instead of one in a neighborhood that already has a myriad of recreational and cultural opportunities.

Democracy in its best public policy sense means participation in a process that is deliberative, participatory, and open. In the urban planning process, this is often meant to include citizen participation in the decision-making process as a way of ensuring that the politicians and bureaucrats making decisions are informed as to the opinions and interests of the residents who will be impacted by these decisions. Particularly in the 1960s and 1970s, the call for "community control" became a rallying cry for urban activists. The need for community input is particularly urgent if the decision-makers are perceived to be from a "sharply different social strata from those affected by their decisions." Including the communities in the process by which decisions are made is a laudable public policy goal, but is often still criticized on the basis that it becomes a way to further middle-class interests while neglecting those of the poor. In addition, minority communities of any composition do not have monolithic viewpoints, and community activists may not always represent the interests of the community more broadly, but rather may represent a tiny but vocal minority of interests. In general, however, institutionalizing the pathways for community participation promotes more open and democratic decision-making, and can result in more knowledgeable government decision-making by providing urban policy makers with a sense of community interests.

Diversity can be a tricky term in any context, and this complexity is not alleviated in the context of urban planning. However, as Fainstein notes, "Diversity is convenient shorthand, encompasses reference to the physical environment as well as social relations, and refers to policy ambitions that go beyond encouraging acceptance of others to include the social composition of places." That is to say, diversity should include both diversity in the use of physical space, and the diversity of the social mix found in these places. Diversity in the urban context should be construed as broadly as possible. A true Citizen City includes welcoming diversity in race and ethnic background, religion, income levels, physical ability, age, size and composition of households, and sexual identity and orientation.

"Inclusivity" provides a descriptive umbrella for encompassing all of these laudable values in a normative vision of urban planning in providing equity by including all urban inhabitants in the vision of – and ability to live in – a Citizen City. Inclusivity must be integrated with the democratic process and represent individuals within that process while welcoming diversity of all kinds by insisting on

inclusivity in urban communities and spaces. Furthermore, this inclusivity naturally creates a more just and vibrant city that can lead to greater social and cultural sustainability.

Sustainability is a broad term that has evolved over time to include social and cultural sustainability. An oft-cited definition of sustainable development is "development that meets the needs of the present without compromising the ability of future generations to meet their own needs." This definition emerged as part of the United Nations' 1987 Brundtland Report. The definition inherently contains the pressing need for environmental sustainability but the report also discusses social imperatives like health and poverty reduction. By 1992, at the World Commission on Environment and Development meeting, the concept of social sustainability was expanded by discussions of components like social justice, local participation in development, healthy environment, safety, and access to education. Cultural sustainability is a more recently added pillar to the larger sustainability discussion and is largely viewed as an extension of social sustainability. It is typically thought to include access to – and preservation of – cultural resources, recognition of cultural heritage including human-built objects, and such abstract qualities as creativity and "a sense of place." Ideally, cultural sustainability should include cultural vitality and diversity, cultural landscape and heritage, and cultural creation, access, and participation.

Engaging all sectors of society in working towards a more inclusive city that generates cultural vitality and access as well as a feeling of community and a "sense of place" is the objective of a Citizen City.

Gould, Marya Cotten. "What Is a Citizen City?" In *Citizen City*, 1–5. Vancouver, BC: Blue Imprint, 2016.

"To take a leading role in contemporary issues, the architect of the 21st century must be a social activist, a realist, a poet, a political technician, and a utopian."

— Alberto Pérez-Gómez

GHETTO

GHETTO
Sanctuary

A Refugee Story

Through the eyes of the refugee, GHETTO is a narrative that depicts how an Iranian refugee family resettling in Venice, Italy converges with an American tourist family on a Venetian holiday. As the refugee narrative progresses toward its tourist sister-narrative (begin at reverse cover), it illustrates the GHETTO's embrace of free refugees into an inclusive community and how their engagement with the American family enriches the lives of all concerned.

Refugee Narrative

Read Right to Left
Begin at Black Cover

Manifesto

Tourist Narrative

Read Left to Right
Begin at White Cover

Passengers, we are passing under the Rialto Bridge.

THE GHETTO

This is your sanctuary where you can begin a new life.

I ♥ VENICE

Welcome to GHETTO. I will be your case manager.

Whoa.

You must be Laleh.

Uh...Yes?

Oh...Thank you, but I am fine here.

Your case manager told you someone will show you around, right?

Well, here I am. I'm Azar.

Come on, the others are waiting!

Look, one day you will want to have a life here and you will thank me.

Hey! What are you doing?

My favorite art installation!

hmm...

≈huuu≈

Gasp

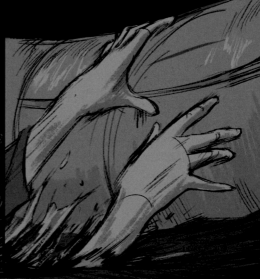

It's okay, just breathe in... breathe out...

Breathe in... Breathe out...

Laleh, are you okay?

≥huuu...≤

≥huuuu...≤

≥huuu...≤

≥huuu≤ ≥huuu≤ ≥huuu≤ ≥huu huu≤

They are too happy.

They didn't go through what we went through.

Exactly.

You know, when I first got here, I hated tourists.

And it's exhausting to keep telling myself that I don't have to be scared anymore.

I hated them because they aren't scared shitless and I was...

...I still am.

Oh, hello.

Aren't you... gonna get in?

The pool water is great!

Hey!

If it isn't Tyler's new friend.

I was thinking of chilling by the side of the pool. I'd love some company.

You know what?

≥huuu...≤

≥huuu...≤

But sometimes, out of nowhere, something will throw me into a panic attack.

My nightmares have disappeared...

I know I have been quiet...This is all new to me, but I think I am ready to share.

I hope I can be here for all of you the way that you've been there for me.

I've been in our group therapy sessions for some time now...

I can't express how much it has meant to me.

Hello!

They will be here soon!

Dinner is almost ready.

Thank you so much for having us.

Welcome to GHETTO.

Flight 8849 to Newark will depart from gate G7...

GHETTO is one-of a-kind...

I forgot how traveling makes me see things differently...

This is your sanctuary where you can begin a new life.

...how separated we are here at home.

I didn't realize...